C

My Single Parent

Julie Murray

Abdo Kids Junior
is an Imprint of Abdo Kids
abdobooks.com

Abdo
THIS IS MY FAMILY
Kids

abdobooks.com

Published by Abdo Kids, a division of ABDO, P.O. Box 398166, Minneapolis, Minnesota 55439.
Copyright © 2021 by Abdo Consulting Group, Inc. International copyrights reserved in all countries.
No part of this book may be reproduced in any form without written permission from the publisher.
Abdo Kids Junior™ is a trademark and logo of Abdo Kids.

Printed in the United States of America, North Mankato, Minnesota.

052020

092020

THIS BOOK CONTAINS
RECYCLED MATERIALS

Photo Credits: iStock, Shutterstock

Production Contributors: Teddy Borth, Jennie Forsberg, Grace Hansen

Design Contributors: Candice Keimig, Pakou Moua, Dorothy Toth

Library of Congress Control Number: 2019955561
Publisher's Cataloging-in-Publication Data

Names: Murray, Julie, author.

Title: My single parent / by Julie Murray

Description: Minneapolis, Minnesota : Abdo Kids, 2021 | Series: This is my family | Includes online
    resources and index.

Identifiers: ISBN 9781098202231 (lib. bdg.) | ISBN 9781644943915 (pbk.) | ISBN 9781098203214 (ebook)
    | ISBN 9781098203702 (Read-to-Me ebook)

Subjects: LCSH: Families--Juvenile literature. | Single-parent families--Juvenile literature. | Children of
    single parents--Juvenile literature. | Parent and child--Juvenile literature. | Families--Social aspects—
    Juvenile literature.

Classification: DDC 306.85--dc23

Table of Contents

My Single Parent

Many families have a **single** parent.

A **single** parent lives alone
with their child or children.

Betty lives with her dad. They do the dishes together.

Amy lives with her mom.

They read a book.

11

Sometimes other people help the family.

12

Kyle's uncle drives him

to **practice**.

14

Nora's dad has to work. Her grandma makes dinner.

Jeff's aunt helps with homework.

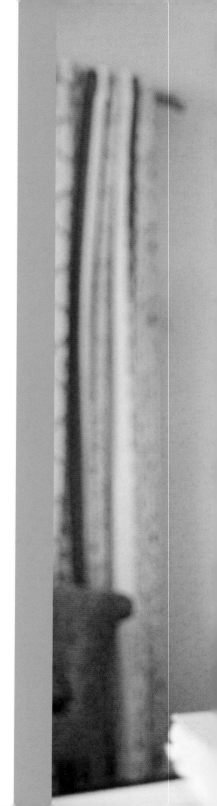

19

Ava hugs her mom. She loves her family!

More Single-Parent Families

Glossary

practice
the time put aside for an individual or a team to become better at a sport or activity.

single
a person who is solely, legally responsible for a child or children.

Index

Abdo Kids ONLINE
FREE! ONLINE MULTIMEDIA RESOURCES

Visit **abdokids.com** to access crafts, games, videos, and more!

Use Abdo Kids code

TMK2231

or scan this QR code!